Adoration

"I am the Way," said Jesus
Only One Way to God
and it is He, a Person…
not an idea, not a work,
not a creed.

Martha Kilpatrick

This is the author's Statement of Faith:

Jesus Christ, the only begotten Son of God,
came in the flesh, shed His Holy Blood on the
Cross at Calvary for the sins of the world.
He is Lord of the Universe, King of Kings.

... and I am His Shulamite.

I will praise You, O Lord, with my whole heart;
I will show forth
(recount and tell aloud)
all Your marvellous works and wonderful deeds!

Psalm 9:1
Amplified Bible

SeedSowers Publishing
P.O. Box 3317
Jacksonville, FL 32206
800.228.2665

Contents

The Anointing

Epilogue

**He who made them
at the beginning
made them male and female**

Matthew 19:4

This is a book about a woman…

       but it is not a book *for* women.
       It is a book for all who seek the Savior.

Sons are called, as are daughters,
       to the place of Holy Bowing,
         at His feet,
      with Mary, your sister.

And the state of Holy Intimacy,
       leaning on His breast
       like John, your brother.

The Word of His Life

The Bible was never meant to be reduced to mere study
nor insulted by dissection.

The Bible is living and… designed to be *lived*.

It is a personal adventure.
By the intensity of living under God's Inquisitive Light,
the Bible becomes the discovery of reality,
not a collection of facts.

All God's dealings with us have their counterpart in scripture
and we walk in the very footsteps of the
characters of the Bible and
enter the stage of their story.

Their struggles are our struggles and
their successes hide our key.

So we comprehend the heroes only when we
fight our battles and find the victory.

We are near to the fallen when
we stare hard at our own stumbling.

The Biblical characters are to be our intimate mentors,
and we, their humble students.

The quest is to find your current path and
your present companion
in the intricate caverns of Scripture.

Then we know God as He really is,
knowable and touchable,
blazingly *for* us but
staunch in
His Unwavering Holiness and
His Glorious Plan...

Introduction

The Bible presents many major truths in twos,
contrasting one against the other...
by this, revealing more.

Mary and Martha are such a juxtaposition.

They cannot be explained by the distinctions of
temperament or personality.
They do not stand for alternative ways to follow God:

"This way or that way,
whichever suits you best."

Mary and Martha, symbols of choice...
between what gains God
against what loses Him.

We defend in Martha that which Jesus condemned.
This only proves that we are... Marthas,
independent and unheeding of **His will,**
dealing only with **our** preference...
Just as she was.

Two roads of choice:
    An open road of comfortable width,
        pleasing to humanity and
    an austere path, gated and obscure.

Only **one way** leads to God and
        "there are few who find it."

Matthew 7,13,14

Bethany

When Jesus visits
some stare but are blind,
some know and are ignorant.
But occasionally one sees
                    in holy wonder…

Ministry Of The Feet

Mary was always found at Jesus' feet.

She sat at His feet for instruction.
She fell at His feet in suffering.
She anointed His feet for burial.
She wiped His feet in gratitude.

The complete life encounter of God, here sketched,
drawn and colored on Mary's experience.

Feet are the most common part of us.
We are grand and glorious creations,
but feet remind us we are all commonplace,
on level ground.
Feet are just for gripping earth and moving.
Nothing nobler can they do.

Feet are humble, touching the earth and, yes, representing that
common reality. The rest of us can float in grandiosity,
but there are the ignoble feet, living in the grimy real.

Before Christ washed the feet of His closest followers,
Mary washed His feet.
Only the two Marys and Jesus were washers of feet.
Of all who followed she embraced this
"ministry of the feet."

Just a strip of leather separated Jewish feet
        from the endless dust of that barren land,
           and often there was no sandal…
           just bare feet touching stone and earth.

Washing feet; the lowest job for the lowliest servant.
        No one ambitious for this job…
           Smelly, thankless… dirty.

But this was her place, treasured and sought.
        Not merely her position or work,
           but her reality… the blank truth about her *self*.

        Mary's lowly humanity could do nothing more.
        Feet were her job.
        Unashamed and willing,
           she performed it with joy.

We must be what we are.
        We must take the place appropriate to **who** we are.
Mary touched the earth,
        not better than earth, but connected,
           having come out of it.

By this fundamental truth she agreed to be,
             simply be…
                     her ordinary self.
In doing so she embraced the Divine Idea of her
      and found the gift of dignity
            that set her individuality apart
               from the common.

The great irony of the universe is this:
        those who lower themselves to the
           earthy mud of their origins
               – *can touch heaven.*

God made mankind out of dust.
     We ever lie and claw to be more,
         another species really,
         anything but common humanity…

But dirt and spit we are…
      and only the vessel willing to be earthen is fit
      to embody the Great Treasure –
          by emptiness of presumption.

To *be* "feet" is the walk, the lowly way to Him.

Seated at His feet Mary heard mysteries.
    Bowing at His feet she saw death destroyed.
        Anointing His feet she was given an exaltation…
            unequal to any other.

When we take our spiritual place at His feet,
    He can take His rightful place as King
        to bestow the might and treasure of His throne…

We democratic people transfer our right-of-vote
        into the Kingdom of God.
This Kingdom is not a republic but rather a Monarchy,
    made palatable by the perfection of its King
        and made just by the all-knowing of its Ruler.

One who sits at His feet has crowned Him
    and enjoys the Unseen Kingdom
        of His Absolute Reign
            and Supreme Protection…

Our ministry to Him must always begin,
    must daily begin, at His feet.
        In absolute surrender,
        a posture of humility before Him.
        We become His feet.

Seated at His feet, we become!
Only at His feet… being His feet are we elevated…
only there can we become
His hallowed hand…
His delivering influence…

We are His feet on this earth,
He, our head, seated on the Throne of the Universe,
We, His literal body – seated at His feet.
We function as the earthly part of Him.
We **are** His feet!
But never under His feet, trampled and crushed.

Feet are the story of the gospel –
the Very Son of God walked the dirty earth among us.

Now we are to walk His earth,
on beautiful feet shod with the gospel…

We are to walk as ordinary people
infused with an Extraordinary God.

The way to God is ever down, He takes care of "up."

The Samaritan

There was a house where Jesus felt at home. His friends in that
house were a family: Lazarus, Martha and Mary.
Each one, a story told forever.

But before the story, we look at its placement.
Scripture has its certain order and that order tells
another dimension to the story,
makes its secret known.

The story appears to begin in Luke 10:38 in the village of
Bethany, but is really birthed in verse 21
at the rejection of two cities who did not believe in Jesus and
were not impressed with his miracles.
In response, Jesus "rejoiced and gloried in the Holy
Spirit and said, 'I thank You, Father Lord of Heaven and earth,
that you have concealed these things from the *wise
and understanding and learned,* and revealed them to babes
(the childish, unskilled and untaught). Yes, Father, for
such was your gracious will and choice and good pleasure.'"

Luke 10:21 Amplified Bible
(Italics mine)

The passage states in principle what Mary illustrates in life.

Martha shows us the self-wise from whom
His life was hidden
and Mary is the child, unveiled and simple,
to whom He was revealed.

Next a lawyer came to test Him with a question.
        "Teacher, what shall I do to inherit eternal life?"
Jesus always made the deceitful
        answer their own question.
Knowing the lawyer was testing Him on
    adherence to the law,
        He asked, "What is written in the law?"

The lawyer answered with the first and second commandments:
"You shall love the Lord your God with all your heart, with all
your soul, with all your strength, and with all your mind, and
your neighbor as yourself."
        Then Jesus told a parable, a story with hidden meaning
           to illustrate the question
           "Who is my neighbor?"

We call the parable "the Good Samaritan."
        A man "fell among thieves, who stripped him of his
clothing; wounded him, and departed, leaving him half dead."
        A priest and a Levite both passed him by
           in revulsion, unwilling to help,
           leaving him to die!

But the Samaritan "went to him and bandaged his wounds,
pouring on oil and wine, and setting him on his own animal, he
brought him to an inn and took care of him."

A parable is a puzzle you must solve,
      meant to send you back on a search for God.

A parable is a question of you rather than an answer for you.
      Yet hidden like a seed of gold
      in the dark soil of the story is
      your answer, profound and wonderful.

The parable is a truth disguised as a story
      that appears to be one thing but means something else.
This story tells of a good person,
      helping the helpless.
And so it has been interpreted through the ages.
      The epitome of a good neighbor.

And that's a fine view… but the real meaning,
      hidden and precious is this:

The fallen man is Christ and the description of
      His crucifixion.
HE was stripped of his clothes, *HE* was wounded.
      HE was left for dead.

The Samaritan stands for the one who will stop life and
      minister to Jesus, ever anointing Him for His
continuing suffering at the hands of the
      ignorant and willful…
            by caring about His cares.

But please note the warning in the story:
> the one who takes the place of the Samaritan will always
be an outsider to the religious, offensive to the legal
> > just as He was...

After this parable, Jesus went to the home of Mary and Martha
and thus began the living illustration – in Mary –
> of the *command*: love God
> and the *parable*: anoint Him for His wounds.
> Mary, by love for Him, was the Samaritan
> anointing His wounds
> > *before* He was wounded.

Many Things

*"Martha, Martha, you are worried and troubled about
many things…"*

Jesus stopped at Bethany one day and Martha bustled to fix his
lunch and make him comfortable.
> She chose to relate to his humanity…
>> Martha would feed Him.

Mary stilled herself in homage before Him.
> She chose to relate to His divinity…
>> Mary would feed *on* Him.

On the stage of her loud performance, Martha complained
to Jesus. Mary was not working and Jesus was ordered to
correct her.

> Jesus is always commandeered to obey those
>> who *work for* him,
> but those who sit in abasement at His feet….
>> let Him be *Himself.*

So the stunning contrast of the two women stands to
> teach us what He likes.
> And what He *does not* like.

To make a noisy display of your labors is to perform
> for the audience of humanity.

A true servant demands no help,
shuns attention.

Jesus' correction of Martha in the Greek language implies
a sharp and severe rebuke. She was wrong. Period.

We are so steeped in the error of working FOR God that
we are determined to defend Martha.
In straining to give her some due, some merit
we are defending our own self-conscious labors
and hoping they too will count with God.
They will not.

Make no mistake, Jesus scolded Martha.

Martha's life was multiple,
dispersed in the fever of many attractions,
confused by many self-loves.
Mary's life was simple,
honed and distilled to
the sole thing she deemed essential,
her object of love, One other than... herself.

Life is a set of enticing traps. A hundred friendly roads
beckon us, promising magic destinations. But to follow
so many avenues creates only a "maze," a futile puzzle with
no escape and no purpose,
and that splendid mystery of our existence is lost by
meaningless circling.

Life is not a number of roads, of avenues to explore.
      And life is not about activities.
Life is a *set of values,* that – if not chosen carefully – descend
      into slavery to the demands of the ridiculous.

Martha lived by roads and activities, not deliberate values.
Jesus diagnosed her – not as productive nor responsible, not
as noble nor even as right. He commended nothing that she
was doing. Do you understand? Nothing!
His dry-boned portrayal of her pointless life was this:
      "you are worried and troubled about many things."

      If you live with 'many things,'
            worry and upset is your living habit.

      Conversely, if "worry and upset" is your habit
            it's a sign you are in the torture of 'many things.'
            Many roads. Many ambitions.

Work is a sorry god whose reward is always strangely empty.
It never pays the wage of love that is anticipated. Yet our faith in
that god is not discouraged by its dead proffer.
We still feed it our highest concentration and our
      finest energy
            though it devours… always more.

Living to work, living FOR work – pays only
      sour bewilderment because
         God is not impressed.

Any fool can spin and call it "noble work."
Mindless labor, even horses do.

Work is humanity's measure of a person's worth.
He is weighed on the scale of productivity and
the more he slaves, the more significant he is reckoned.

The more he can be a martyr to labor, the more sympathy
or admiration he gains and
that brief attention is his final wage.
But it is pay that buys... nothing for tomorrow.

Martha's work was meant to gain acclaim and
earn His attention.
She was buying His admiration,
paying for His love.
But He was not for sale and
she felt cheated.

So she thought she would help Him see...

Her petulant "Lord do You not care?" was
the whine of self pity and a shameless insult to His love!
It was Martha who did not care... about Him.

We are always exposed by how we accuse God.

The Choice

" Mary has chosen what is better." NIV

Jesus explained the difference
        "Mary has chosen," He said.

Nothing complex, nothing difficult,
        the answer was very, very simple.
                Not that Mary was indifferent, ungodly or lazy.
                Not that Mary had it easier...

Just this:

Mary chose... and she had chosen... ***Him***.

This explained her activity that
        Martha counted as inactivity.
This was the outward result of her secret motivation,
        the point of her power to bow, to hear, to see and
            most of all... to be still.

        Her power was from her choice.

In the midst of possibilities, of different opportunities, of
myriad options, Mary had chosen Him as her highest treasure,
her goal, that which was important enough to let
        all other importances simply... go.

Not that Mary could choose and poor Martha,
being too caught up in mundane duties
had no time or chance to choose.
No, Martha had chosen duty and Mary had chosen Jesus,
and Mary's choice was presented as superior.
"Mary has chosen what is better."

What you choose takes you over and compels you.
Your resolve is so powerful that it forms its own
highway and drives you toward its arrival.
Once your choice is made you do not steer.
It steers you.

You are owned by your decisions.

You find yourself the slave of your choices and
that is either bondage or joy...

Martha endured a contorted misery.
Mary enjoyed a bliss of stillness.

You are today what you chose yesterday.
Choice may seem unconscious, but it is never so.
Choice is always deliberate.

Choosing can be casual, floating lazily with the tide.
Indecision is a decision-to-not-decide
and as such... rules.
Decision leads us.
You choose. You always choose.

Volition is the force, the power, the drive
     God supports and calls the heavens to sustain.

Free will is a gift distinguishing us from all creation.
       God gives that gift and will not rescind it.
    He offers utmost respect to our intention.
       Would that we gave it such regard ourselves.

Would that we understood the terrible power,
     the oft' irrevocable consequences of adverse choice.
         Our own choice!

Not what is "done to us,"
not what is outside our control
      but what is awesomely *within* our parameters,
     what we ourselves direct in secret
         through preferences we will, or desires
           we *elect* to support.

That immense power of decision takes us over.
     You are today what you chose yesterday.
     You have lost today what was not willed yesterday.
     You will have tomorrow what you elect today.

We flow in the constant undammed stream of
our unwitting choices and cannot swim against that tide.
     Its strong current is set by
         our willing and by our desiring.
We are always eating fruit from the
          seed of our secret intentions.

Yet, we stubbornly believe we are ineffective victims
in a universe that opposes our best efforts.

This is certain: Opposition does meet every decision.
Mary was opposed by family,
but Martha was opposed by God Himself.

Your choice chooses your opponent, but have one, you will.

Do you see?

You are free to choose but only choosing the "one thing" –
that which is "better" – brings you to rest and
the intervening defense of a Shielding God who takes on
your petty adversaries… all by Himself.

One Thing

Jesus added insult to Martha's injury.
He pointed to her sister as the example of His pleasure.

> *"…but only one thing is needed.*
> *Mary has chosen what is better…"*
>
> Luke 10:42 NIV

One thing? Among all "things?"
    What is the one thing better than all other things?
        What makes all the others irrelevant?
    Surrender at His feet? A subservient slave?
        No, He wants friends, not vassals.
    Reverence for His stature?
        No, He wants lovers, not monuments.

He wants ones who will give their inner world,
        surmount their intellect,
        diminish their independence
        for the sole purpose of ***being with Him.***

Mary had one stark and vital agenda.
                And that was… no agenda.
All the purposes were His to originate.
            Any activity was for Him to command.
She drew up to Him in intimate bowing,
        close enough to hear – if nothing else –
        His breathing.

In her brazen awareness of Him,
>
> every desire and every focus was centered on Him.
>
>> **On Him**, *alone.*

Mary never gave in to the fray that was swirling around her.
>
> Her concentration unbroken by the criticism,
>
> she never entered the fight her stance had created.

What was the **one thing?**
>
>> Others found it as well.

David said, "**One thing** I ask of the Lord,
This is what I seek: that I may dwell in the house of the Lord all
the days of my life, to gaze upon the beauty of the
Lord and to seek Him in His temple." Ps. 27:4 NIV

Paul also. "…I consider everything a loss compared to
the surpassing greatness of knowing Christ Jesus my Lord,
>
> for whose sake I have **lost all things**."
>
>> Phil.3:8 NIV (Emphasis mine)

There are ones who want to know Him more than they want
to know… anything.

Those who boil and distill their lives down
>
> to the bare bone of
>
>> Jesus in whom they find all the fascination
>> they can handle.

And these are ones with whom He sits.

The Welcome

*"… JESUS came to a village where a woman named
Martha opened her home to Him.
She had a sister called Mary, who sat at the Lord's feet
listening to what He said."* NIV

Mary, defined only by her relationship to Martha as "her
sister," was placed under the eclipse of Martha's driving energy.
But Mary moved to sit in Another's shadow.
She took her place on the floor.

Mary received Him.

Martha only welcomed Him…
with loud applause and perhaps flamboyant pride.
He, the famous, came to her house.
It was spoken of as *her* house.

The proud deign to give by conspicuous generosity.
The humble – aware only of gaunt poverty –
sit down to beg.

We have nothing to say to God but thank you.
No place to give Him but a home in our heart.
No gift to offer but ***unguarded receptivity.***

Mary received Him… into life's only two treasures:
her heart and her time.
This was her house.

She gave Him the space to be Himself,
>to define – reveal – His Own Splendid Being.

No others did that, not even the disciples who wanted
>Him for the super hero of their imagination.

To Mary, He gave His secrets.
>Busy little beavers building dams of safe protection,
>>have no time to woo His secrets from Him.

In the end, Martha found Him to be a
painful interruption of her contrivance –
>an ungrateful intruder into her very soul.
>She did not want to be perceived by God,
>>only by man.

It was really only Mary who gave Him the open invitation
>to His own dominion.

It was after all… *His* house.

The Work

A valid work waits for us:
    A work of God's design.
        A labor calling for courage,
          a sweating toil that is
              our greatest adventure.

Jesus answered
        the valid question of responsible men
"Tell us how to work the works of God."
      "Work," He said is this: "To believe in the One
        He has sent..." John 6:29 NIV
          and that is most practical.

Believe that the Son of God is
    your very performance, your duties,
      your strength to live.

Another lives your life... entirely. Does your work
      for you... instead OF you.
    Another Energy moves you.
    An entirely Other Life propels you,
    and that Other Being completes your tasks.

The work to attain this is the investment in a relationship.
    Mary's unacclaimed labor:
        to build a relationship with the Son of God and
            from that deep kinship –
                to believe in Him.
                Live BY Him.

To build a union with the knowable Son is work,
        requiring all the energy and focus
           of any other toil.

It takes an exertion of the blank will
        to meet God face to face.

Activity can shield you from it, spare you and
protect you from that Awful Gaze
        on your ugly nothingness.

Activity can mask an empty soul and give you a fake
        costume of nobility.

But to face God when He calls your name
        takes more grit than mere toil,
           more sweat than projects.

And to care for nothing except Him – no one but Him –
        is a reduction that means labor
           unto very death.

Mary did it. She worked to subdue her mind to His mind,
        her life to His wishes,
        her time to His pleasure,
        her heart to His love.
Mary's secret work – by being hidden –
        gained no accolades from her peers.

To listen to One outside yourself,
to hear a Voice that has no echo – because not audible –
        is the hardest work of mankind.
        So hard that few will do it.

It means waiting, it means risking. It takes a surrender of every
device, the loss of every independence.

The normal work of humanity is increase, but
the labor of spiritual listening is only decrease.

To listen to a Divine Intellect so beyond us that it is foreign
to every space of our comprehension
        – to listen to That Voice –
        is to do the deliberate work of making oneself stupid,
                crippling one's own ego.
        And that is work *against* your "self,"
           the other work, *for* your "self."

Listening to anything outside of our self-absorbed notions is
hard labor, but to listen to God requires
> the loss of intellectual liberty
> to fathom a Higher Intelligence.

Mary, reduced to a life of listening,
> learned to hear nothing else.

The common opinions about Jesus went past her.
> The current gossip of His exploits did not capture her.
> The doubts, the slander – she was simply uninterested.

> Even to her own family's disdain,
> she wouldn't listen.

The awareness of her whole being – mind, heart and body –
> was engaged,

> seized by a Divine Fascination
> that made the very world disappear...

The Person

God became a person. God indwelling His own creation!
He who made us, walking around as one of *us*...
Amazing!

Since we could not unite with Him –
born dead by Adam's fall,
He constricted Himself
to our realm... to be discovered.

He is reachable now. He is personal.
But we still leave Him alone on His distant throne,
push Him back to abide in the categories of our dogma –
"remote and uninvolved."
We practice life in front of Him
but keep Him far from our passions.

God is willing to be and wants to be
(Do you understand? He *wants* to be!!)
the Intimate Companion of the most secret place,
the Consummate Lover to the desperate soul.

To Mary, Jesus was a person – fabulous and amazing.
She knew Him by His name... **JESUS**.

He was not just Teacher, Rabbi, Father.
He was a person, knowable, intrinsic.
          He was not His labels… to her.
      He was not His roles,
         He was not even His miracles to her.

He was her *heart's* companion,
     the long-lost mate to her soul, the finishing
     of her own being, the mirror of her creation,
       the secret of her mystery.

She let Him into her ordinary humanity
        with no inhibitions.
She exposed her bare soul to Him,
        to be known, to be captured.

By such unveiled access, she enjoyed *rapport with God!*
Perhaps it was that rapport to which Martha really objected,
        and not the housework at all.
        It does raise the ire of watchers.

Mary moved in a relationship,
       comfortable and private,
       so intimate that He was her world,
       a literal realm in which she lived,
         secluded within His Presence.

He came to earth to be known, not *used....*
to be perceived by His own exquisite character,
and she was the first to profoundly value
His Real Identity.

As God, we acknowledge Jesus,
but as One who had lived as a Person,
human, normal, accessible –
and now empathetic to the lowest of our
human baseness –
this we cannot imagine!

That would be too, too good!

The Conflict

Mary and Martha stand for a principle.
They are real but at once also…
symbolic.

They are flesh and spirit. Two ways to live. Two powers within.
At war, at enmity, they cannot both rule. And they will not
coexist for they are not compatible.

One or the other
must be given mastery.

Flesh is Martha's vain delusion: "I know it. I can do it."
Spirit is Mary's instinctive reality:
"I don't know it, I can't do it. O God!"

In God's family, Flesh become workers and
Spirit are worshipers.

Conflict seethes between them, insolvable
because irreconcilable.
You cannot work *for* God and worship Him
at the same time.

Worship concedes that God is everything while work is
humanity helping Him in His inadequacy.
The workers have contempt for the worshipers and
forever pit themselves against that occupation.

The worshipers have no such contempt for the workers
because they have no interest.
They are too enmeshed in the adventure.

The principle – which is *the* mortal problem –
is as old as the scriptures.
Mary and Martha are Cain and Abel.

God rejects the offering of work, the labor of the fields.
It is self sufficiency, independence
and these are actually… defiance.

Lift up the stone of any human achievement and
you will find that every "good work"
hides an eventual death.

Cain brought his fruit of sweat and diligence.
Abel watched the flock. They just grazed and grew
by God's enabling.

Cain offered his precious produce, a tiresome creation
of his own for which he claimed proud credit.
Abel gave back to God what God Himself had done.
A life offering of blood.

And just as happened to Martha,
Cain's tedious offering earned… rejection.

The terrible injustice of that inflamed him.
So Cain shed innocent blood, his brother's.
Offering to God can be only blood. He has thus decreed it,
and it cannot be overruled by human superiority to
God's All Knowing Wisdom.

If you will not offer God blood, then you will shed blood…
by a revenge against God played out on Abels who do.
Blood is inevitable in dealing with God,
and it will be spilled either by obedience or by rebellion.

Workers murder worshipers
in one form or another…

Many are the biblical Marys and Marthas, cast by
dissimilarity into ageless conflict.
Isaac and Ishmael. Ishmael, wild and furious, fought
for his provision.
Isaac meditated in the fields and all things
came to him by gifting and inheritance,
without striving.

Saul and David.
Moses and Joshua…

Moses, the weary leader, by enormous
effort and monumental patience never
entered Canaan, the land of rest.

What took Moses (Martha) 40 years at which to fail,
took Joshua (Mary) 11 days to succeed.

Joshua let God be God – walked in,
crossed over, conquered – rested.
Not ever easy. Sometimes not clean…
but always God. Only God.

Mary and Martha are
compelling – and competing – drives within us.
Both live and make their presence known by inner
pressure. And they constitute a crisis of choice.
The selection is entirely secret… and internal.
Which one will dominate?
Which drive will I nurture, allow to take me?

Struggle is the natural road of arrogance.
It can be the feverish work to do *something*
or the lazy quest to be *somebody*.

Worship is the more instinctive need.
To *worship work* is the mixture of ruin
but is the relentless temptation of our nature.

The conflict is eternal… with eternal repercussions.
The choice is… a **forever** one.

Known

To know about God is one thing
     but to be "known" by Him,
          ah, that is the bliss of Mary.

*"...but if one loves God truly (with affectionate reverence,
prompt obedience, and grateful recognition of His
blessing), he is **known by God** (recognized as worthy of
His intimacy and love, and he is owned by Him)."*
               Amplified Bible I Cor.8:3
               (Emphasis mine)

You know Him by being known,
     by letting His invasion have you,
     by having a house with no doors
          and windows all open.

And as you look in the mirror of His gaze
     you see your true self – by His vision...
His perception being the only true knowledge
          of your enigmatic self.

In His boundless imagination, He dreamed your being and
     created you to a divine specific.
        The Designer knows His design...

He also knows how far your meddling has
     marred the original.
          All this is seen in seeing Him…
               looking up and out,
                    sitting at His feet.

In that place of surrendered silence, all He knows of you –
     and of Himself – becomes your secret, too.

The Need

The contrast of the two is drawn,
  deliberately placing one beside the other,
  seeing each more clearly
    in the other's reflection.

Martha marched in her self sufficiency,
  Mary nested in her *insufficiency*.

Mary's direction was set by her abject need.
Her motivation was powerful, fueled by her desperation.
She knelt because she needed Him,
  she chose because she required Him...
    as her Supreme Necessity.

She did not choose because she "knew" to choose.
  She chose because she was honest enough to
    live her innate poverty.
  Choice was the *result* of her need.
    Choice wasn't her noble decision,
      made in the wake of her superiority.

No, it was comfortable inferiority
  by virtue of raw necessity.
Her need of Him was joy... no embarrassment of nakedness,
  no shame over dire want.

Mary accepted her severe human void
     with all its pain and humiliation and
       filled it only with
         Jesus… her completion.

Her barren soul recognized He was her Existence.
Her hungry heart believed He was her Sustenance.
Her questing mind knew He was her Reality.

Mary let her emptiness be.
    Martha filled her void with… herself

Mary listened because she was
     desperate to hear.
   Martha *did not* sit at His feet because
       she did not *need* to hear Him!

Need is the great gift of God.
While He let us choose our independence of Him in Eden,
   He did not release us from needing Him,
   and that necessity *for* Him is the route back to Him.

Need is the screaming crisis of our core:
     the abject, groveling need of… God.
     And *nothing* – no attainment and no person
      will fill that
      groaning cavity.

But it is a nightmare to be forgotten, a specter
too shocking to face, too disturbing to admit.
It is this we hide even from ourselves,
      that raw primal need,
        the naked vulnerability we ever clothe.

All humanity lies in mutual consent to conceal this
     inner bankruptcy.
        We validate each other's mask.
        "If you don't admit it, I won't."

But the honest beggar ponders alone,
     "It must be only me.
     You do not seem to have this same
        embarrassing cavern of inadequacy."

Poverty of spirit is a thorny ally,
        an embarrassing companion,
who – if you befriend – will lead you into the Kingdom
      that is the place of your opulent belonging.

Mary sprawled in utter contentment with
      her blatant destitution and
        it unhinged the onlookers.

There is only one principle of the kingdom: **receiving**.
ALL has been given.
Read the Book and see.

But only the hungry receive food.
The sick alone take in the cure.
And only the needy are filled.

Live comfortably with your terrible need,
surrender your lonely self to it…
then you can receive.

When you can receive, it is instant supply
because "it is finished."

And then you have everything… you need.

In Him!

One Possession

"Which will not be taken away from her…"

Mary's choice secured her the one possession… described as
permanent and untouchable.

Nothing that can be named or touched is enduring.
    And nothing is "mine."
    There is nothing
        – no position, no place, no item, no fame –
           that is stable, secure, reliable.

No person is "mine…"
    Not those who come from my body,
      not those who vow covenant with me,
      not even those who choose to be mine.
    They can be taken from me by powers beyond me –
        before which… my helplessness is total.

I can cement no relationship. I can protect nothing.
I have no *power* to own. I have no capacity to keep.

What I clutch, I kill. What I want, I cannot capture.
What I seek to possess, betrays me by the capture of me.

All good things of people and treasure may enter my life,
      but nothing has my title on it,
      nor my security in it.
        Nothing is "mine."

The true truth is that I have
Nothing and No One.

All is loaned, seasonal, passing...

We live on borrowed time, in temporary places,
            with fleeting activities.
All of life is a fragile thread, a flickering wick,
            passing through with nothing remaining.
We know this in the depths of our frightened souls,
            and all of history proves it.

He calls for me to leave all for His sake.
Lands, houses, family, loves –
            but His call is to leave only
            an illusion of security,
            the fantasy of being chief
            by the presumption of an earth-given right,
            on the basis of some burnable piece of paper:
            deed, birth certificate, marriage record,
                        citizenship, family tree.

His call is total – even to the abandonment of my
            ownership of *me.*
    I cannot keep my health, my sanity, my perceptions.
And it is simply a call to true reality, the blank truth that
                none of these are mine,
a call to leave the presumptuous ownership of that which
            I have never really owned.

In this terrifying humanity that is
               bound to a corrupted world,
               we need permanence,

       something not subject to human tyranny and ruin,
       something untouchable by nature's heavings.

By desperation we will create this security by proprietorship.
          "Mine! Do not touch!"

We paste together our little domain of pebbles
             and call it "Home,"
        a safeguard immovable and imperishable.
        We rest in the shadow
            of its false cover and
               lie to ourselves about its safety.

We need a Rock, not subject to
      injustice nor susceptible to destitution.
      This is pure human need by virtue of utter weakness.
      For all our false bravado, we are squalling infants,
         helpless and naked.

The Rock is God. Irreducible. Indivisible.
         He is the Only Solid amidst all things fluid…
The Solitary Refuge that is able to protect
         because He is the Only One
         who controls, owns and manages ALL.

"The earth is the Lord's and the fullness thereof…
and they who dwell therein."

Nothing and No One exists *for* me. All is God's and all exists
to serve His Idea… of which I am simply one.

All ownership, ALL *rights* of ownership are God's.

He has purchased all by the price of costly Sacred Blood.
He has every legal right to His property.
We, the cruel usurpers of His domain.

I can have All and Only… God.
He is All I have – truly the only possession possible.
But He is ALL I need and the Only One I require…
And *that* is permanence – unchanging, immovable.

God is mine. "I will be your God."
His own statement of permission
for my clinging grip to possess Him,
a pledge to my absolute "right" to
His presence in my days.

I cannot overstep my need of Him.
I cannot demand too much of Him.
His rule is absolute but under that rule,
He has committed
His entire realm to my hungry disposal.

If I am His, then He is mine… and all that is His, is mine.

God has withheld nothing. "If He gave His Only Son will
          He not also freely give us all things?"
In owning nothing but God, I own all that He owns.
                    And that is… All.

What Mary chose to seek… to grasp… to own –
          possessed her and also became the Treasured Property
                    to which she gained permanent title.

Christ was her personal Wealth, her Prize of Life, her Home.
Neither man nor nature could move or remove this possession.

                    No evil could dislodge it. No enemy steal it.
                         He, the only Imperishable, was
                              the hiding place of her spirit.
                         And no one could get in, much less steal.

If you are His, God is yours.
          And what is His becomes yours,
                    there to clothe your naked existence and
                         sustain your marvelous destiny –
                              by HIS wealth.

          What is released into His ownership becomes
                    His private, surrounded property.
          And all His Massive Power is given to
                    its care and utter safety.

He gives *Himself.* Do you understand? *Himself!*
               without reserve,
         to the absolute end of your need,
                from the now of a common existence
                through an unfathomable eternity.

Lazarus' Tomb

Stinking death and decay are only
rags that fall off in Jesus' presence
when He calls *your* name.

The Village

"Now a man named Lazarus was sick. He was from
Bethany, the village of Mary and her sister Martha."
John 11:1 NIV

The village… now listed as Mary's.
    It had been Martha's house.
    The stakes of her turf clearly driven…
        but it was Mary's village.
    She had no fence nor boundary.
      Jesus was her home,
      she had no other.

Obsessive work confines you to the circle where
your labor lives, a cage of limitation.
    Martha's life was walled.
    Mary – unbound – free of "place,"
      moved in a larger world.

Mary, by making Jesus her centrality,
became herself the center of her watching world…
                  as we shall see.

Christ is the pivot of history, the crux of every matter
    and when He is the core of your story,
      you become the unconscious center of your world,
        a focus for the puzzled.

"…many Jews had come to Martha and Mary to
comfort them in the loss of their brother."

"When the Jews who had been with Mary in the house,
comforting her, noticed how quickly she got up and
went out,
they followed her….
supposing she was going to the tomb to mourn there."
John 11:19, 31 NIV

The mourners from Jerusalem stayed with the
grieving women.
When Martha marched to confront Jesus,
they stayed with Mary.

Martha met Him alone, no audience.
She who wanted an audience, played to the crowd,
had no interested spectators.

But when He summoned Mary, they followed her.

Marthas glean respect. We think well of them.
But they inspire no fascination and evoke no mystery.

We do not approve of Marys but we cannot
stop watching them!
They live in some exquisite sphere unknown to us.

Where Marys go, adventure goes. When Martha went she
had doctrinal conversation… and the dead stayed dead
        but when Mary went… the dead *lived!*

Influence can never be conscious.
        If it is conscious it is manipulation and not *inspiration.*

Marys draw followers who love her love. But she is largely
        unaware and even ignorant of her appeal.

        The power of influence is a scent rather than a speech,
                a mystery instead of an explanation.

David was a Mary. Even in his shameful exile,
                followers flocked to him
        in the fierce loyalty of love for him –
        and by that love willing to share the
                deadly danger in which he lived.

The world disapproves of Mary but
                cannot shake her magnetism.
The world of people praises Martha but
                knows she holds no mystery.
        Who wants to follow acid tongues
                and trite complaining?

Martha gave the world her efforts and labors,
and the world was bored.
Mary inadvertently showed the world Christ
and they were captivated.

Those watchers had no fascination for Martha even when
she left to meet the Savior.
But just to watch Mary cry at the tomb,
that was enough to stir them to move.

Love Without Favorites

"Now Jesus loved Martha and her sister and Lazarus."
John 11:5

The love of Christ is indiscriminate. He loves all.
Jesus loved Martha.
His correction did not diminish nor disprove that.
His love is total for every person.

He loves because He loves.
He does not love because of anything.
He loves you for no reason. You'll never give Him one.

Martha here is mentioned first. Mary, minimized;
that He loved her was obvious.
Martha, unlovable, was loved the same.
And that Love for her, confronted and rebuked.
Why? Because He wanted her love as well as Mary's.

Her feverish labor kept her from the very
love she was trying to earn.
He loved too much to leave
that alone and let her have her noble delusion.
Her error cost her HIM but it also cost HIM... her.

In the rebuke of the Lord,
> love is never in crisis, never threatened.
His love is a constant, a love we cannot
> destroy by our misguided pursuit of it,
> > nor our foolish avoidance of it.

The passion of His reprimand, obvious in the Greek language,
revealed the anguish she caused Him!

We never think He is affected by our wanderings.
> We see Him as though He were like us.
> > "What do I matter?"
But we wreck His heart and tear His Holy Soul by
> trying to win what He longs to give.
> By resisting His reach of love to lasso us in.

God's love and His pleasure are two different things,
> unconnected because unrelated.

While Mary pleased Him by her choice of Him,
> Martha was set on her path of futility
> and it troubled the Lord.

So Jesus invaded her commotion to clear for her
> the vision of a different road.

The Love of God is such that
    He will guide us while we fight Him,
    and keep the option of choosing Him ever open.
    Such is the kindness and commitment of Divine Love
        which is not changed in the slightest by
            our failure to love Him and...

    even the blindness to see that we do not.

Knowing All

Martha marched to confront the tardy Jesus as He strolled
toward Bethany. She, bold of accusation, would have Him
explain till she was satisfied.
       He should give account of His failure.

She engaged Him in a sort of doctrinal argument which His
       graciousness accepted.
    He meets us where we will meet Him
    but ever pleads to move us to His higher ground.

Before He could speak, she said *"I know… God will
    give you whatever you ask."*

By this anticipation of what He *could do,*
      she demanded what He *should do.*
      It was a subtle command
      of Jesus to perform, not a faith that He would.
      The presumption of the Marthas who
        order God to do what He does.

First Jesus gave her the personal promise:
    "Your brother will rise again."

To which she answered, *"I know,"* for a second time.

Martha used a word for "know" in the Greek (oida) that
meant a complete knowledge, a finished understanding.
It was a word for her intellect,
        her mental knowledge of truth.
The door of her hearing was closed
           for she already knew all.

Paul never used that word in referring to the Lord.
His word for "know" was "ginoska,"
one that meant an ongoing, unending revelation.

Martha's logic led her.
Her mind was where she related to Jesus and
        He could only meet her there.
        So He did, but ever calling her to
        move from knowledge to relationship.
           To see Him!
        By His identity to commune with Him.

God cannot be known nor captured by comprehension.

No labels please. He will blow them away, or worse,
        let you have them.

Jesus is a perpetual mystery, a constant surprise.
        He was not predictable nor understandable.
        He can only be followed, never anticipated.
        He cannot be led. He is Himself a Follower.
           All His paths are original.
             Even so, now…

As a last attempt, Jesus told her who He was, a new
revelation He had given to no one before this.

> *"I AM the resurrection and the life. He who*
> *believes though he may die; he shall live, and*
> *whoever lives and believes in Me shall never die.*
> *Do you believe this?"*

Willing always to speak His treasures to the deaf, He proved
how He valued her, how He longed for her to know…
Him, not about… Him.

You are teachable only when you are destitute,
when your questions have no answers.
And you listen only when you need answers.
Martha was not teachable… she had no questions
so she had no quest.

Again Martha asserted, *"Yes, Lord, I believe that you are the*
Christ, the Son of God, who is come into the world."

"And after she had said these things, she went her way…"

Marthas have the last word, even with God.
And her last word was a truth that — by her actions proved —
she did not comprehend that which she did not hear.
But she resolutely believed… she believed.

It is possible to see who Christ is without any
           connection to Him…
      to believe without faith,
      to follow without surrender,
      to be of Him but not with Him.

To recognize who He is without the
           comprehension of what it is you know.

To know volumes and remain completely ignorant…

      Especially about God.

Waiting For The Lord

"When Martha heard that Jesus was coming, she went out to meet him, but Mary stayed at home."

John11:20 NIV

Martha rushed to meet Jesus before He even got to Bethany.
    Mary stayed at home.

You would have thought it would be the reverse…
Mary ever seeking Him, deeply aware of Him –
    surely she would be the one who flew to
        Him in trouble.

Marthas go where they are not bidden, answer when they are
not asked,
        initiate what God did not begin.
      Marys, yielded even in crisis, wait till sent for…
       Surrender to His orders without ordering Him.

Jesus did the same, not moving toward Bethany for days
    until His Father bid Him,
      even though He knew Lazarus was dead.

Mary, in knowing Him, knew His ways.
    She could only wait for His summons.
    She, by gazing at Him, had become like Him.

"(Martha) called her sister Mary aside. 'The Teacher is here,'
she said, 'and is asking for you.'
When Mary heard this she got up quickly and went to him."

Martha named Him Teacher, a Greek word that meant
     Instructor, an ironic title for her,
          as she was not one taught.

For Mary He was Lord and Lover, not teacher.
     But because He
          was Lord, she waited until sent for.

     Submission is the response of love to Being Loved.

The Dead Stink

As Jesus approached the tomb of Lazarus,
she to whom He promised life,
to whom He revealed Himself as Life and Resurrection,
    made the ludicrous assumption that
    He did not know the dead stink!

"Martha... said to Him, 'Lord, by this time there is a stench,
for he has been dead four days.'"
John 11:39

He who created life and filled the universe,
    who knew all the past as well as the startling
        future of the man... knew that
        Lazarus was in the stink of decay.

Marthas are ever educating God.
    "Poor God, He needs my help.
He doesn't understand. Let me tell Him what is going on."

She who believed she believed and even proclaimed,
        "I believe" had no faith in the actual and
        no clue of His intentions or His power.
What she believed about this Lord of Life
    were simply lofty ideas about some distant future
        with no reality for the present.

Knowledge is always future… therefore dead for the now.
That's safe. No error there, but…
Faith is current and viable for it is grappling with
the urgency of today.

Faith that raises the dead never rises from
the reasonings of a religious mind.

True faith grows in the realm of the heart
by the catalyst of Love.

Jesus Wept

"Now Martha said to Jesus,
'Lord, if you had been here,
my brother would not have died.'"

"Mary came… fell down at His feet, saying to Him,
'Lord, if you had been here,
my brother would not have died.'"

There is a vast difference between
    a petulant complaint that reprimands God
    and a stunned quest to fathom Him.

The initial words of Mary and Martha were identical,
    the difference lay in the hidden heart
    which Christ alone can discern.
    He never answered words,
    only hearts.

In His presence Martha stood and Mary fell and thus
    revealed the difference in their hearts.

To the calloused heart He always
        answered questions with questions,
            making a person declare their error
            out loud in the hope that
            they would hear themselves, if not Him.
                This He did with Martha.

The relationship of Jesus and Martha existed
    only in ideas and words,
        a liaison merely of the mind.

To the vulnerable heart of unveiled passion,
    He gave – not only answers – but miracles of action.
    To the soft heart, His own heart replies.

Martha engaged Him in truth but Mary captured His
    heart by the influence of her anguished
        submission in grief… sprawled at His feet.

So Mary, by her surrender of bewilderment,
    ignited the compassion of His divinity.

She said only one sentence,
    no argument, no discussion.
    She simply came to Him because…
        He was the Solution.
        To everything.
        To anything.

His heart was torn by union with her heart
    and His soul wept with her in the silence of their
        profound intimacy.
He gave no words of answer…
    Their communion was not in words,
        their closeness needed no
            conversation that others could overhear.

*"Therefore, when Jesus saw her weeping... He groaned in
the spirit and was troubled."*

No Answer! No Words! Do you understand?
    His entire Holy Being was
        wrenched in intimate fusion with her suffering
        and He moved to demolish the laws of death.

He turned from Mary with His spirit
    heaving in a travail of intercession
    and asked that the tomb be opened.

The Word of His Power called one name and death fell
        off the corpse.

    Lazarus rose alive out of a consummate death,
        old and putrid.
    Hopeless, but for the plea of love to the Source of Life.

    In response to Martha, He explained.
    In response to Mary, He raised Lazarus.

I would rather move Him than understand him.

I would desire to wring my broken heart before Him
    than exercise my mind about Him.

I would prefer to be ignorant and in the desperation of
    bewildered love
      than informed and... blind.

Following Mary

"Then many of the Jews who had come to Mary,
and had seen the things Jesus did, believed in Him."
John 11:45

Mary, the pivot of the story – she the one around whom
the miraculous occurred. Because the people stayed
with her, they saw *and...* they believed.

Marthas beget Marthas. And Marys birth Marys.

When Mary ran to Jesus in answer to His summons,
the Jews went with her. They hadn't followed
when Martha went out.

We may sympathize with a complainer,
we may think they are right, but
we'd just as soon let them go on by.

When Mary moved, they moved – behind her.
They did not approve of her. They did not comprehend her,
but they smelled life and hope, and they were
inexplicably drawn.

They saw her lavish love for Him,
igniting the countenance meant for Him alone...
and they followed.

When she stayed, they stayed.
    Where she went, they went also.

And because they followed her, they watched Jesus master
    the unimaginable and so met the One Mary knew.

    And they too... believed.

The Anointing

Jesus is still being sold and used,
and even now, rarely anointed
by the understanding of His followers…

Two Days

In less than a week – just two days,
                Jesus would be crucified and
                He was moving toward
Jerusalem for that awful appointment with His purpose.
                Consider His state of dread.
                Think about His thoughts!
                Gethsemane's resolving had not yet come.

Yet there gathered around him in normalcy,
        a supper of His friends and disciples.
        Lazarus was there at the table and Martha was serving.

Things were going on as usual.
        No one believed in His crucifixion.
        He was the Son of God! Sent to rule the nation.
        Death, unthinkable.
        Jesus did not know what He was talking about!
        Crucifixion, indeed!

The supper was given in the home of Simon the leper,
a man healed by the very Master who sat at his table.
        But it held a peculiar and secret poignancy for Jesus.
        Simon was the father of Judas Iscariot.[1]

It cannot be imagined – the depth of Jesus' blank horror.
        He knew His traitor all along.
        Yet here He sat, guest in his home, healer of his father.
        Soon to be murdered at his hand.

[1] John 12:4

Eating and serving, talking and laughing. No one noticed
the soberness of Jesus, nor cared for His quiet needs.

While others had been about their humanity's doings
            and pleasures at Martha's house,
        Mary had listened at His feet to the
                subject of His anguish,
                    the coming Cross.

No one heard Him but Mary. She, the only
        friend to HIS need, believed that
        whatever He said was truer than any
                truth she knew.
He was going to die… soon… and horribly.

And her servant's heart was ripped by what He
        faced. While all others ate in comfort
        and spilled their precious final hours,
                she thrashed and wept.
        How, O how to comfort Him?

Broken Vessels

"...a woman came having an alabaster flask...
Then she broke the flask and poured it on His head."
Mark 14:3

Saving nothing, holding back no part,
Mary broke the alabaster jar,
itself a treasure, spoiled for any
future use.
It was for Jesus, no other use
would it ever see. All for Him.

Mary broke her beautiful jar, but that
was nothing for she
took her own being, heart and soul
and broke it before Him for His use.

Her gift merely a picture of her life,
opened by the brutal choice
of self annihilation,
her own secret death for Him
to Jesus, her Love,
her Only Love.

Mary acted out before Him His own crucifixion.
The bottle shattered – His broken body.
The contents poured out – His Holy blood spilled.
She understood and she showed Him...

It was about His death but
            it was also her own death to lose him.
          She was ministering to Him but
     she was also consenting to say goodbye
          to her Greatest Necessity because that
                was His will… and desire…

She would support His choice at
          the expense of her own needy existence.

No more would she sit at His feet and
            hear His heart's secrets.
     Never again see His glowing face, nor hear His
     loving words, not ever, ever again feel
           His piercing touch.
     He was going to the Father, by deliberate choice
     and that meant as well, leaving her behind.

To let Him go would have been a great sacrifice
          but to help Him in it, to sustain His going…
          ah, that was the truly broken vessel.

          Compared to this,
          the alabaster jar was nothing.

Costly Oil

*"A woman came to Him having an alabaster flask
of very costly fragrant oil, and she poured it on
His head as He sat at the table."*
Matthew 26:7

"…a pound of very costly oil of spikenard"
John 12: 3

Lazarus and his two sisters were poor,
                they had no servant in the kitchen.

       Mary had one treasure, worth a year's wages.
                Set aside to save,
                       her precious wealth.

She took it from its hiding place.
        She knew now what He needed.

She would not fight His dying as did Peter.
She wanted what He wanted. So she would
        send her heart with Him into
                this gruesome ordeal.

This oil of spikenard, a whole pound.
        Give some? A part… no, it must be all,

               "for He is all to me."

Scorned and rebuked,
　　she walked past her cruel critics.

In the grip of a passion that made her
　　　　immune to their disdain,
Mary poured the oil on his head so that
　　　　it spilled down His body,
　　　　splashed it on His feet and
　　　　as a final brazen statement,

　　unfurled her hair, a thing not done in public,
　　and wiped His feet with it.

　　Blatant intimacy for a
　　　　conspicuous anointing...

　　　　Outrageous deed,
too extravagant for the approval of decent people.

His Worth

"But there were some who were indignant among
themselves
and said, 'Why was this fragrant oil wasted?
For it could have been… given to the poor.'

And they criticized her sharply."
Mark 14:4,5

What you give to Christ is precisely
    the measure of His worth to you…

How much you give, what you give up,
    how much you keep,
    these tell the story of His secret merit to you,
    and… the gauge of your love.

At one place or another, by this way or that
He asks for every treasure on this earth because
    that is the test
    not only of your obedience but of
    His esteem within your secret heart.

He is Himself the jewel above rubies,
    the treasure in the field, the pearl of great price.
    The most valuable being in the entire universe,
    His worth – inestimable.

To possess Him costs to the last thread of all
        hoarded property, be it
        land, loves, or luxuries.
        For some, their very blood.

Eternity will prove His worth and the utter foolishness
        of any other prize.

We will either pour out all our treasure to Him,
        or spill our eternity in the waste of
        all His goodness.

To purchase you from the prison of sin
        cost Him all,
        even His place with His Father.
To be worthy of His payment and His presence
        (though not to earn it, for it is done)
        you also must pay the full price,
           pour out your treasure to the last
           drop of costly oil.

Mary had given Him two treasures:
        her time and her reputation.

Now she gave Him in just one extravagant moment,
        that which cost a year's wages to earn.

This is the picture Mary drew for all of time.
    The picture of His worth,
        not just to give all to him but
            to participate in His Cross
        by love for Him.

      The Lamb *is* worthy.

Waste

To the foolish giving of
        what was not necessary,
        nor even appropriate –
the disciples objected by moral indignation.

"Why this waste?"

Leaping to their proud assessment with sharp criticism,
      the disciples did not dream they had crudely exposed
          the level of their regard for Christ.

Judas protested for the sake of the poor,
      from whom he stole money.

Simon, a man healed of leprosy, the disease of rebellion,
      Not only healed, forgiven.
Even he did not defend the esteem of Jesus.

A waste is when you give a juicy steak to a dog.
      A dog is not worth it.

Waste is giving a pearl to swine, throwing gold into the sea.
      Waste is giving something of value to
          that which has not a comparable worth.

To no one there – not even his own disciples –
      was Jesus worth a year's wages.
      Only to Mary.

Jesus' value is inestimable. How could we calculate
His worth and value to God, yet God wasted Him
on us, breaking the vessel of His body
and spilling
Him out by His own Holy Blood,
poured out on the ground of a polluted earth to
cover the filth of our impurity,
His innocence for our guilt.

There is nothing – no gift, no amount of sacrifice –
that could ever be
a waste poured on Him!

Fragrance

"The house was filled with the
fragrance of the oil."

Mary poured the excessive oil on Jesus' head.
　　A pound of perfumed oil, a huge bottle.
Down it flowed, soaking His hair and beard,
　　saturating his clothes, covering His skin
　　　　the way oil adheres…

　　It was a literal bath in this sweet oil
　　　　and the fragrance was so strong
　　　　that it "filled the house."

　　She knelt down and covered His feet with it
　　　　and wiped the excess with her hair.
　　Mary gave Him her scent.
　　The adoration of a human for its Creator.

And the oil she poured on Jesus
　　　　spilled on her, clung to her hair.
　　　　She smelled as He smelled.
　　　　And He smelled as she smelled.

Such is the aroma of
　　　　a life lived for His wishes.

　　Made one, an aroma to God, pleasing and satisfying.

And He took it with Him, smelling of her ointment,
down the shouting streets of Jerusalem,
into Pilate's court of wrongful trial.
Before the contemptuous scorn of the Pharisees,
He wore her love in the fragrance that
clung to Him.

Through the beatings and bloody lashes
still that scent lingered on him.

As they drove the nails, the guards would have smelled that
oil covering His skin as the sole comfort
in an experience filled only with malicious hatred.
As He hung on the cross, did that odor give Him
comfort and hope?
Did He know that at least one loved Him?
and that many also would?

Did His skin, soaked with blood, still smell of
oil of spikenard?
Could He smell it in the hours He hung there
suffering with the load of our sin?
By then an odor, faint and fading, but He...
still anointed with the incense
of that loving worship,
a symbol and promise of the ones
for whom He was dying.

He was naked – wearing that anointing as
             His only covering –
  a burning sacrifice unto God,
          pleasing and sweet smelling.
The soldiers, fighting for His scented robe,
      cast lots for that garment,
          soaked with holy oil of Mary's love.

     The oil would have spread among them
             as they took it from Him for their own.
     His last earthly possession except for the oil that
          clung to His skin.

He said! HE said, she has anointed me for my burial.
     He said, "She has kept this for the day of my burial."

As He lay in the tomb, unadorned with spices.
     It was too late for that – He was adorned.
     Anointed with the lavish Love of Mary by her sacrifice.

And God, who asks for fragrance and
     who dwells where the incense of sacrifice wafts
    before His holy nostrils, was drawn back to
the scented body of His forsaken Son, lying dead in that
     cave, but still smelling of the oil of spikenard…
             by Mary's hand.

And He was, by that same oiled body, raised from
    death to a new form of life we will one day share.

    Does He wear that fragrance still?
    Is it a scent we will absorb when we see Him?

Many have smelled in this life,
    a sweet odor of His presence.
  Is it that very oil, always clinging to Him, even now?

Does it still give Him the promise of all
    the future Marys who would make His
    dreadful suffering worth it...

     lovers not servants,

     but by love, made... servants?

Memorial

*"Assuredly, I say to you, wherever this gospel is preached in
the whole world, what this woman has done will also be told
as a memorial to her."*
Matthew 26:13 and Mark 14:9

The deed of Mary, so strange, so inappropriate,
  (in the middle of dinner?)
    condemned by those
  who had no place in their heart for Jesus' needs.

Jesus, moved profoundly by her poignant grasp
  of His coming death,
    lifted this deed to the place of
    an eternal memorial.

Linked forever to the gospel,
    exalted by Him, as no other event
      in the Bible.

This deed we ***must*** understand.
    It is His Emphatic Command
    to always present this story where
      the Good News is preached.

    The question is: Does this act speak to me in the
        core of my salvation as
      part of the simple redemptive plan of Christ?
          Is it memorialized in me?

What is the meaning of Mary's act?

The disciples raised a smug defense of humanity's need.
"It should have been given to the poor."
Their certainty was that Christ existed *for* mankind.
That human crisis was God's obligation
and the first priority for Christ's followers.

They were wrong.

Such is the mistake to which all believers fall prey.
To serve people is the error which ends
their worth to God and the hope of fruit.
Turns them into the bitter slave of human devastation
while certain it is God's will,
sacrificial but heavy, heavy.

It is the error of Martha.

Mary's deed is the sign and symbol for all time of
true ministry – authentic service to God that
brings His glowing approval.

This is the ministry: to serve His Son FIRST by
the dictates of HIS needs.
And those needs cannot be known by presumption,
only in daily profound listening by
the communion of love.

The ancient command says it: Love God with everything
    in you and of you, mind, heart, strength – all.
Only when you've done that – THEN
       love your neighbor as yourself.

The temptation is to believe that to love your neighbor
       is to love God.
    The next logic is that love is to "do" for that neighbor.
No. Love, so intensely defined, so unequivocally demanded by
Jehovah could only be personal and individual
    by the route of an ongoing relationship kept real by
    a full-orbed communication… with God Himself.
       Not humanity's need of God… first.
          But ever second.

God created mankind out of His need! He is complete
    and self sufficient but in His love He NEEDED
    an object by the sheer enormity of that love.
       We are that object.

    You were created for love. You were made BY Love.
      And you were made to NEED love
         and to need TO love…
        and God needs you to be the
        recipient of His love.

As Mary met His need for an intimate companion –
        HIS need, do you hear? –
she was the unknowing catalyst for the world of her
    influence, demonstrating – living out – that the
        way of Christ was *relationship,*
        passionate, free, intense and reckless.

The watching world of the religious did not merely
        disapprove of her oil,
    they really were repulsed as well by
        her radical love for the Master.

    But somewhere in us all is the inherent vision
    of just such a Divine Adoration and we are given both
        hope and despair at the sight of it.
          The hope to possess it,
          the despair that another does.
    A terrible fate would be to never *witness* it.
An even worse fate would be to never **experience** it.

"God so loved the world that He GAVE his only Son…"
    but the Son came because He loved the Father!
      Jesus lived for, died for the love
        He had for the Father,
        not mankind… first.

As He loved the Father and His life of obedience was
a ministry always to what the Father
wanted and therefore needed,
so Mary's was a pattern of that,
the first human pattern following after
Jesus, in the New Testament Story.

But thankfully, not the last.
The disciples also came into her pattern of Jesus' pattern.
And a few, since.

The anointing of Jesus is
the living portrait of ministry that must
go out with the Gospel.
The motivation of love for God that spills one's life
out before Him for
whatever purpose **He** needs…

And please note, it is a memorial not to Himself,
but to HER.

"If anyone serves Me, Him My Father will honor."
John 12:26b

Judas

"Then Judas Iscariot, one of the twelve, went to the chief priests to betray Him to them. And when they heard it, they were glad, and promised to give him money. So he sought how he might conveniently betray Him."

Mark 14;10,11

There are probably only two ministries in the universe:
anointing His feet or arranging His murder.

Judas watched the anointing and it stirred his jealous hate.
It gave the last resolve to what had been an option.
Something he had long toyed with in his mind now
suddenly was a bold decision.

From that very room, out of the presence of that holy act,
straight he went, crazed and fixed, to
sell Jesus to his murderers.

What did Mary provoke in Judas?

Mary prepared Jesus for His death but Judas orchestrated it.
Close but so far apart.

It was not Judas who was provoked. It was Satan, prince of
hatred for the favored Son of God.

What Mary did in love and what Jesus commended by
    gratitude, incited Satan to a savage madness.
        "It had to be done now!!"
    The puppet of his venom was Judas, duped to
    think the scheme was his.

By dabbling too long with secret blasphemies,
Judas was taken over by the Enemy he entertained.

By musings and reasonings that seemed innocent,
    he lost his soul.

Such rage of hell is always awakened
    by the Marys in their bowed
        worship of the Savior.
For Mary is the worst possible enemy of the Enemy.

Once Love has taken hold, the war is over

        for *only* Love can defeat Hatred.

Epilogue

To see Him, to find Him…
How?
I have a teacher if I will
be her student.

The Defender

For all her opposition, for all the accusation,
Mary never answered, never explained.

And she never deviated from her course.

Not only did Jesus take up her defense,
but in a sense He attacked her attackers
and shamed them by exposure.

She never answered Martha. She never had to.
Jesus defends those who give Him
the place of the One Essential.

He takes up Himself the fight for your rights
and the defense of your actions.
He is the personal advocate for His Marys.

One who is focused only on JESUS
cannot concern himself with himself;
he is not even interested.

And when Jesus defends you, it's all over
for your opponents.

You have won
the war
without a fight.

The Treasure Of Time

Time is the treasure of life. Time IS life.
Time is the willing sacrifice that you offer up to
            the worship of what you love.
Don't tell me what you love. Tell me where you spend your
            TIME and I'll tell YOU what you love.

The dispensing of time, the investment of time
                    is the exposure of what you truly love.
        You give your time to your cherished treasure. You do.

Frenzy says there is no time left for God.
            Hurry cannot live the life of a Mary.

Haste insults HIM. It says there are
other important, more urgent activities than being with
            the Lord of the Universe.

It takes giving Him the costly gift of time to find Him,
        to hear His heart,
            to gain the wisdom of where to spend your
                riches of time.

    Many give their lives to Him,
                    who do not give their *time.*

To the frantic, Mary's life was waste.
        The waste of time and energy on Jesus.

To the busy, time is always critically short.
There is not enough time for the ambitious...and the worried.
　　Their many works are more than their shoulders can
　　　carry, more than their hours can cover.
　　They are like Martha, always behind and
　　　ever in self pity because of it.

　Their efforts are their own.
　　Jesus did not call for them
　　and can not be blamed when the efforts
　　　do not succeed or give fulfillment.

Time is the shining jewel Satan steals.
We do not understand its value as much as he does.
If he can get your time, he has... you... without God.
　　Your time is your life.
　So by noble demands and foolish distractions,
　　he ekes away the minutes of
　　　your eternity.

There is all-out war for your time,
　　a relentless and clever scheme to fill
　　　your days with what is not God –
　　what is not for Him or even about Him.

Martha was the unwitting instrument of that fiendish enemy
to call foolish and irresponsible in Mary what was really...
　　God's highest and best.

Thus it will always be.
There is a fight to be a Mary.
And it takes a strong-hearted resistance
   to defend the preciousness of your own time.

To lose your time is to lose your destiny.
  To squander time is to waste your only wealth.

There is abundant time for your assignment...
  for God's authentic will.

Plenty of time to listen and ample time to accomplish.
  God set the earth on the axis of Time
  and when He rules it,
    it is – like all His gifts – an extravagant supply.

God requires in this day, the offering of time.
  Give time to God and you become rich in Him.
  For to give time is to give your self
  and He gives HIMSELF in return.

God is ever real about time and humanity's limited span.
So whatever is given to Him is multiplied by the mystery of
  His transcendence over Time and Space.
Time given to Him is returned enlarged, expanded by a
  multiplication that cannot be comprehended.

Mary lavished time on Him...
    because she deemed Him worth it.
Martha had no time for Him, only a period to work
    for Him, a labor He
        rejected as a real... waste of time.

To Martha, Jesus was not worthy of her focused attention,
    and this He painfully knew by watching how
        she spent her... *time.*

The Rest Of Mary

Work does not begin with work.
God's work must begin from rest.
It then moves out from rest to
      power and performance.

      Work that does not start with rest is
      work without Christ's approval or
        participation.

Life is confusing, insolvable.
      Pressures of this realm load us up
        with expectations and feverish works.

Need screams your name.
Duty puts strings on your hands and makes a puppet of you.
Affections tie your heart in knots of obligation.

And the temptation is to move, move quickly, so much to do!
     "A crisis! Perform! It is waiting – and I'm the
       only one who can do it!"
Time seems inadequate to cover the task and
      energy, meager for the size of the demand!

Rest is the first step of work, the beginning of
what is a process. To find your particular work
and to shed false labors, takes
> an intense search for your destiny and
> that is only found… in stillness before Him.
> making Jesus Lord and Master – and initiator –
> of your deeds.

Jesus declared His last human words, "It is finished."[1]

In that Divine Declaration,
  the entire human dilemma was solved,
> sin conquered
> death defeated… but these were not
our only two problems! There was also the problem of
> life and life is made up of *work.*

The curse on the ground was broken and
> Jesus Himself solved the human
> > problem of work by
> the most amazing solution!
He would perform our work Himself.
> This is our Sabbath rest.
> He works, we rest.[2]

God's quiet call is simply to come to Him…
> and cease striving.

[1] John 19:30 [2] Romans 5:4

You must unburden before you can take up
     His undistorted burden.
By simply coming, to take off that human load
       and lay it on His Divine Shoulders,
    only then can you bear the Divine Yoke.[1]

Come to Him – sit at His feet and let Him sort through
       the maze of your demands and worries.
       Let Him eliminate what is not yours
       and separate the possible from the irrational.

Rest is a place to live, one to which you
      must return every day,
           because of the wandering human will and
              its propensity to slide into
              ridiculous efforts.[2]

This is the genius of Mary.
       She would not move until she rested with Jesus.
       She refused to be the puppet of human madness.
       Her will was set and fiercely fixed on Him.

          And her calm was the proof of it.
          No one could pressure or shame her out of it.

You have nothing to give TO Him
       until you are filled WITH Him…

[1] Matthew 11:28   [2] Hebrews 4:10

The Sound Of Silence

Mary lived in a profound silence.

In all three episodes she is quiet.
> Only one small quote is recorded.
> And it was a plea directed to Jesus,
> > not for the ears of people.

The message of her life:

> not a legacy of words
> > rather the stark absence of talk,
> > > a silence… rare and mystifying.

The only voice in her life was Jesus'.
He *spoke* for her, *about* her… in *defense* of her.

Mary had no drive to explain,
> no compulsion to be heard.
> no obsession to be understood.

Lust for audiences had been abandoned.
> All such had died in her.

She had found her soul's understanding in Him.
She had been still enough to know she was **heard**
          and now – in quiet –
          she could listen.

Our idea of prayer is to hurl words at God.
      Mary knew prayer as silence in His presence,
          to listen… without the audacity to speak…

*"The Lord is in His Holy Temple, let all the earth
keep silence before Him."*
          Habakkuk 2:20

The world is a swirl of noise,
          a loud competition of voices,
          in piles of useless words.

Mary neither entered it nor heard it.

The only words she strained to hear were the
          captivating Words of God in Christ,
          full of Living Eternity.

      And they were – for her – priceless,
          the only Words worth hearing.

Silence is one thing – amazing in itself –
    but stillness is a rare internal quiet
        a peace of the mind,
        a rest of the heart,
    by having found one's long lost home…
        in the Soft Presence of God.

Mary found serenity *before* she entered stillness.
    True quiet issues from inviting God into
        the long-sealed chambers of the soul
        and letting His invasion calm
        our native hysteria.

Self-centered talk is the expression of pride,
    of not having seen the
        God whose Face perceives us.

Meekness is not natural to a humanity
    that thinks it is
    superior to its own Creator.

Humility is the quality of having had
    vain illusions cremated by
    the Burning Love of Christ.

Silence is born of humility,
    the awareness that you have
    out of your self-taught ideas
        nothing to speak worth hearing.

It is having encountered
     God by His True Size
breathtaking and magnificent
     and seeing the
contrast between you and Him.

It is the *exact* measure of
     your consciousness
     of God and the
proof of your confidence in Him…

     that He really IS…
          the God you want Him to be,
          nothing less and so much more.

We do not grasp the Holy Gentleness of God.

If we insist on
     the babble of our crude humanity,
     charmed by the sound of
          our own noise, then

this God of Kindness will stand back,
     robed in His Tranquil Dignity
     and let us have the vain spotlight
          of endless talk.

His voice is not in storm or wind,
        not in earthquake nor fire.
We could not bear that voice in
        the Fullness of such Measureless Energy.

    As Elijah learned, His voice was still and small,
        "delicate and whispering."[1]

    Jesus said to His disciples, "What you hear
        whispered in your ear…"[2]

    If humanness will merely be still,
        The entire Trinity will come forth
        and speak
        by a whisper in the silence…
        heard by no one else.

[1] I Kings 19:12
[2] Matthew 10:27 NAS

The Gaze Of The Soul

Mary filled her sight with Jesus. The eye of her being
    had no double vision,
      seeing the world and God... both.

She saw with concentration, one Object,
    the Important,
        ignoring the unimportant.

The gaze of her inner soul, fixed on Him,
    held no competing vision.

The eye of your soul is not in physical sight.
    It is the focus of *thoughts*,
      the obsession of the heart... in secret.

Where your eye is turned is the
    certain direction of all your future.
        What you see is what you follow.
        Where you look is where you go.
        The object of your focus is even...
            what you become.

Humanity is always consumed with something,
      riveted to some internal essence.
Our nature is devotion –
creatures of worship, bowing subjects
    to something chosen,
      worthy of love.

The eye of human nature is fixed
      in sick infatuation with
            the unworthy object of… *self*

Mary gathered the fragments of her
      scattered sanity,
          left the complexity of logic,
          the endless boredom of her
              predictable self
          and in simplicity, with single focus
          gazed on Jesus.

The seeing of her mind,
      the center of her heart
          was a Person, not an idea,
          not a doctrine
          nor a religion.

As David of old, she had
      formed her purpose
      to seek after Him,
      to know Him intimately,
          by a passionate choice
      to "behold the beauty of the Lord."
                         Psalm 27:4

To fill her being with
      consideration of One
      other than her all-demanding self.

She had found One whose mystery
      held her imagination captive
         and there was no reason
         to look in any other direction.

"If your eye be single,
      your whole body will be
         filled with light."

                        Matthew 6:22

And she was.

Mary The Child

Mary is the child, "to whom the Father reveals His secrets."
She is the 'child' who enters easily, the kingdom of heaven.

By subtractions she lived, not addition, nor
                complex multiplication.
      Drastic reduction of adult la-de-dah,
      abandonment of competition,
      the unloading of arrogant responsibility
      and disinterest in the pretension of importance.

Adults live in the future or the past,
      sometimes both,
      ever trying to fix the mess.

Mary, oblivious to the mess, just as a child would be,
      lived in the wonder of the moment.
Now – the only reality that held her fascination.

      Everything was "this moment" for Mary,
            all work, errors and problems.
      And that made her
            fresh,
                current,
                    unencumbered.

      No past and no future.
      Only the exquisite now.

Childlikeness is not child*ish*ness.
>Childlike is the simplicity of utter honesty,
>>spontaneous and true, pledged to whatever *is* true.

>Childish is flawed character,
>>escaping the real responsibility
>>of living in pure unmasked existence,
>>>true to self and real with God.

Martha was the 'childish', playing adult scripts,
>tedious and pompous.
>Boring ambition –
>>self conscious and uninspiring.

Mary, the child, lived creatively in her primitive self
>without sophistry.
>That was her simplicity.
>>She was natural, but not naive.

The true child lives by the innate discipline of two things:
>its own uninhibited passion and
>>the desire to please the Parent.

Mary –
>willing to be nothing
>>in worldly importance,
>>>honored in an eternal emphasis.

Nothing, being nothing!
Being ***nothing***.
Being nothing…

           that is a child,
       whose significance lies
               in God alone.

A Simple Love

Mary loved Him.
>That's the entire explanation of her.

Many witnessed, heard, were healed by Him…
>but never loved Him.

Myriads study, read, recite and mimic Him today…
>but never love Him.

She, the illustration of the first commandment.
>By His First Command God revealed Himself
>>…and His need.

To Love Him with all – that is her mark, her identity,
>and her eternal fame.

And it can be the legacy of those who comprehend her.

So we must know her secret.
>We must know how she came to love Him.

Mary let herself need Him by naked desperation.
She received Him and let Him be her Savior.
>She let Him wrench her heart
>>with the shock of sin.

She let His love burn into her heart
until she loved Him...
"because He first loved her."
Let! The magic word, the simple key is let...
a word of non resistance,
open surrender.

In all the world and universe, of all who have lived
and ever will live,
only One Loves, only One.
Mary loved Him with a Love He gave her... Himself!

The first commandment – Love God with all your being,
body (all your strength), soul (all your mind)
and spirit (all your heart).

The amazing, exciting secret of the Gospel is that God
Himself fulfills that commandment to
all who will let Him![1]
The hidden spring of life is your considered opinion of God.
Everything outward, and forward
is determined by this inward.

The central sin of all sins is simply –
the failure to love God.
Because it is God's first order,
breaking it is the essential sin,
the heart-root from which all
other sin is merely a branch.

[1] John 17:26

In the secret marrow of Life's bare bone,
        do you love Him?
The Garden's crisis was a choice –
        and so is yours.
Love God or love self.
Man and woman both became
        self conscious lovers
        of self… made a god.

So now humanity lives unborn and
        hideously inbred
            until God is the
                heart's Lover,
                the soul's Joy,
                and the mind's Rest.

You do not love Him like Mary?
        Do not worry… just choose.
            And He will give you such a love.

Invitation

I can be the chief of Marthas. I was well named
    but by that challenged.
And I have been an ardent pursuer to be a Mary
        to my Christ for almost 30 years.

    So I write… by knowing *both*.

    And I end with an invitation.

To you who do not know Him as Savior but need Him,
    I say, ask… ask and ask again
    Ask Him to give you the repentance
        that is the door to Salvation.
        Ask Him give you a new birth.

To you who are weary with labor for Him,
    and now see there is a way of quiet joy
        sitting at His feet, I say
    simply choose as MARY did.
    and seek Him with all the desire He gives you

…and **HE** will come to *your* village to find you.

Praise To The Author

I cannot dedicate this book to any person for it is HIS,
  from the living to the writing, it is Christ, only Christ.
    'For me to live is Christ'

And I cannot thank a person, for all things come from Him
      and are for Him."Every good and perfect gift is from
above, and comes down from the Father of lights..."

James 1:17

But I wish to exuberantly thank my Lord and my God
    for these, my "good and perfect gifts."

For my husband, Kenneth,
        God's greatest human gift to me.
    Father, bless him forever for his
        love and longsuffering.

For the inexpressible joy of my children,
        Scott and Robyn, Lee and Debbie,
        Sam and Julia... and their golden children.
    Father, overwhelm them with Your Love.

For the rich unity of the Body of Christ,
        the church that He has built among us.
    Praise for each one of you,
        though not named here, known to His heart.
    Father, store up their reward in many crowns.

SeedSowers

Prices as of 2000

REVOLUTIONARY BOOKS ON CHURCH LIFE

How to Meet In Homes *(Edwards)*...10.95
An Open Letter to House Church Leaders *(Edwards)*........................4.00
When the Church Was Led *Only* by Laymen *(Edwards)*.................. 4.00
Beyond Radical *(Edwards)*...5.95
Rethinking Elders *(Edwards)*...9.95
Revolution, The Story of the Early Church *(Edwards)*..................... 8.95
The Silas Diary *(Edwards)*... 9.99
The Titus Diary *(Edwards)*... 8.99
The Timothy Diary *(Edwards)*.. 9.99
Priscilla's Diary *(Edwards)* (2001)... 9.99
Overlooked Christianity *(Edwards)*..14.95

AN INTRODUCTION TO THE DEEPER CHRISTIAN LIFE

Living by the Highest Life *(Edwards)*.. 8.95
The Secret to the Christian Life *(Edwards)*.................................. ....8.95
The Inward Journey *(Edwards)*.. 8.95

CLASSICS ON THE DEEPER CHRISTIAN LIFE

Experiencing the Depths of Jesus Christ *(Guyon)*............................ 8.95
Practicing His Presence *(Lawrence/Laubach)*................................. 8.95
The Spiritual Guide *(Molinos)*.. 8.95
Song of the Bride *(Guyon)*... 9.95
Union With God *(Guyon)*.. 8.95
The Seeking Heart *(Fenelon)*...9.95
Guyon Speaks Again *(Guyon)*... 14.95
Spiritual Torrents *(Guyon)*.. 14.95
The Ultimate Intention *(Fromke)*...11.00

IN A CLASS BY THEMSELVES

The Divine Romance *(Edwards)*... 8.99
The Story of My Life as told by Jesus Christ (Four gospels blended).....14.95
Acts in First-Person... 9.95

THE CHRONICLES OF THE DOOR *(Edwards)*

The Beginning.. 8.99
The Escape... 8.99
The Birth.. 8.99
The Triumph... 8.99
The Return... 8.99

IE WORKS OF T. AUSTIN-SPARKS

)MFORT AND HEALING

THER BOOKS ON CHURCH LIFE

IRISTIAN LIVING

Please write or call for our current catalog:

SeedSowers
P.O. Box 3317
Jacksonville, FL 32206

800-228-2665
www.seedsowers.com

Also by Martha Kilpatrick

All and Only

... a book about God's greatness
and humanity's need of Him.

Order though:

SeedSowers Publishing
800.228.2665
www.seedsowers.com

For tape lists and additional information
please write to:

Martha Kilpatrick
Shulamite Ministries
P.O. Box 10
Suches, Georgia 30572

or call:
1.888.355.5373

Visit us on the web at:
http://www.shulamite.com